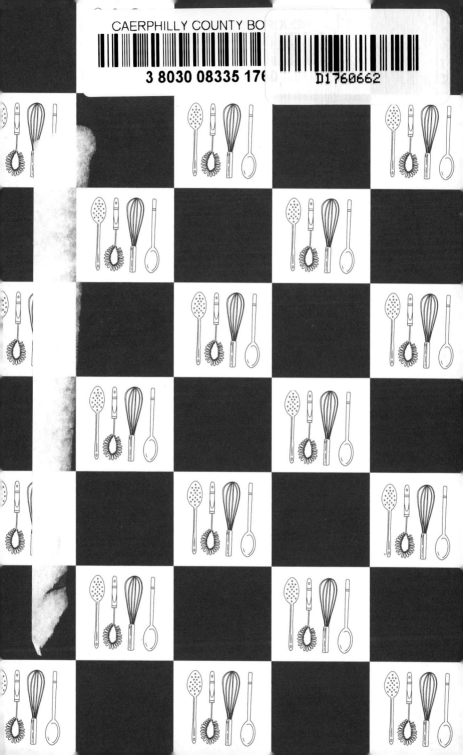

MARVELLOUS MEALS WITH
MINCE

Editor:
Valerie Ferguson

LORENZ BOOKS

Contents

Introduction

Ground or minced meat is versatile, economical, goes a long way and is ideal for any number of quick and easy dishes. Nowadays, the range available from butchers and supermarkets includes chicken, turkey, pork, lamb and even fish, as well as the more usual beef, providing scope for an immense range of both traditional and more unusual dishes. If you have a mincer or food processor, it is easy to make your own mince and prepare other meats, fish and shellfish that are not commercially available.

This book is packed with ideas for family meals, snacks and light lunches, kids' dishes and even special occasions. Recipes range from traditional family favourites to more exotic dishes and include pies, fritters, pasta and stuffed vegetables.

Ground meat combines well with many other ingredients, from herbs and spices to cheese and creamy sauces. No wonder it features in the cooking of countries across the world, many of which have inspired the recipes in this book.

Whether you are planning a midweek family supper, entertaining on a budget or tempting kids to try new dishes, one of the many recipes here will provide the solution.

Ingredients

Beef

This is the most widely available and popular type of ground meat. Obtainable in different grades, the most expensive is usually the leanest. Some supermarkets supply extra lean or premium quality mince, but these terms have no legal meaning. Cheaper mince usually has a higher fat content – up to about 25 per cent total and about 12 per cent saturated. It is, therefore, of poorer nutritional quality and a false economy. Minced meat dries out quickly, so use it on the same day it is bought or freeze it immediately. Ideally, buy steak in a single piece and mince it yourself.

Below: Robust flavours like chilli, pepper and bay are idea for minced beef dishes.

Pork

Very popular in many central European recipes, ground pork is often mixed with other types of mince, elsewhere pork is used less frequently. It is usually taken from one of the forequarter cuts and as this is comparatively lean, it is ideal for a meat loaf or stuffing vegetables. If a fattier cut is required for a terrine, for example, it is better to buy belly pork and mince it yourself.

Lamb

This is widely available and second to beef in popularity, especially in Middle-Eastern recipes. It is usually taken from the neck, breast and flank, ideal for fast-cooking burgers and shish kebabs, but avoids a high fat content, it is better to buy the meat in a piece and mince it at home.

Poultry

Virtually interchangeable in recipes, ground chicken and turkey are becoming increasingly popular. The fat content is considerably less than with red meat because most of the fat is removed with the skin. While less strongly flavoured than beef, for example, ground turkey or chicken can be used in most recipes that call for some sort of mince. They should be used on the day of purchase, as they quickly develop a slimy texture and go off rapidly. Grind your own meat from turkey or chicken breast or leg.

Herbs & Spices

Both fresh and dried herbs can be used to enhance the flavour of mince dishes. Italian dishes, such as lasagne, benefit from oregano or marjoram. Basil is also widely used. Parsley and thyme are good-all-purpose herbs. Tarragon is a popular choice for chicken and rosemary is the classic herb for flavouring lamb.

Chilli is essential for Mexican dishes and is used in Indian and South-east Asian cooking. There are a huge number of varieties from fairly mild to fiery hot. You can remove the seeds from fresh chillies for a milder flavour. Chilli powder is also often used in minced meat dishes.

Other popular Indian spices include coriander and cumin. Fresh root ginger is essential for Chinese, South-east Asian and many Indian dishes.

Binding Agents

The most common binding agent in burgers, rissoles and patties is egg but in some Asian recipes cornflour (cornstarch) is used instead.

Store Cupboard Ingredients

Mince is perfect for making use of store cupboard ingredients. These include dried or canned pulses and canned tomatoes. No-need-to-soak dried apricots give lamb a Middle Eastern flavour. Both fresh and dried breadcrumbs can be added as a bulking agent or used to coat rissoles and patties. Other bulking agents include bulgur wheat, rice and oats. Useful store cupboard flavourings are sweet chilli sauce, cranberry sauce, creamed horseradish, mustard, soy sauce and tomato ketchup.

Fresh Ingredients

The range of fresh ingredients that complement ground meat dishes is vast. Aubergines (eggplant) are essential for moussaka and leeks, onions and spring onions go well with all kinds of mince. Mushrooms, carrots and potatoes, as well as other root vegetables, are characteristic of many dishes. Fresh tomatoes are delicious in sauces and good for stuffing, as too are peppers.

Cheese which melts well, such as Cheddar, Parmesan and Mozzarella, makes good toppings. So, too, do yogurt and soured cream.

Below: Chopped onion for flavour and egg for binding are used in meatballs.

Techniques

Mincing or Grinding Meat

Ready ground meats are easily obtainable, but when you want something more unusual or to use a particular cut of meat, you will need to mince it yourself.

With a mince or meat grinder:

1 This produces the most uniform minced meat, and you can choose coarse or fine texture, according to which blade is used. Trim and cut the meat into 4 cm/1½ in cubes or strips before feeding it through the machine.

By hand:

1 Trim the meat. Using a large knife, first cut the meat into cubes, then chop into smaller and smaller cubes. Continue chopping until you have the consistency you want, coarse or fine.

With a food processor:

1 Trim the meat carefully (be sure to remove all gristle because a food processor will chop gristle too) and cut it into cubes. Place in the machine fitted with the metal blade and pulse.

2 In between turning the machine on and off a few times, stir the meat around with a spatula so that it is evenly minced. Care must be taken not to over-process meat to a purée, particularly if making hamburgers as they would be tough and chewy to eat.

Mincing Fish

Fish and prawns are ideal for mincing in a food processor, using the chopping blade.

1 Wash, skin and bone the flesh.

2 Flake the fish and place in a food processor fitted with a chopping blade.

3 Process the fish for 30 seconds on high speed, or until finely minced. Use as required.

Basic Sauté

This cooking method forms the basis of many ground meat recipes. Meat is cooked in a small amount of oil to tenderize and seal in the flavours.

1 Heat a little oil in a heavy-based frying pan over a medium heat for 1 minute.

2 Add the minced meat and sauté gently for 7 minutes.

3 Stir the meat, breaking it up with a wooden spoon, until it is brown and sealed.

Dry frying

An alternative to the basic sauté, dry frying is a healthier way to seal meats as it does not require any additional fat or oil.

1 Heat a non-stick coated frying pan gently over a low heat.

2 Add the mince. Sauté for 5 minutes, stirring and breaking it up with a wooden spoon, until brown and sealed.

Clear Soup with Meatballs

The tiny meatballs not only look attractive in this Indonesian soup, they also make it quite substantial and filling.

Serves 8

INGREDIENTS
175 g/6 oz/1½ cups very finely
    minced (ground) beef
1 small onion, very finely chopped
1–2 garlic cloves, crushed
15 ml/1 tbsp cornflour (cornstarch)
a little egg white, lightly beaten
salt and freshly ground black pepper

FOR THE SOUP
4–6 dried shiitake mushrooms, soaked in
    warm water for 30 minutes
30 ml/2 tbsp groundnut oil
1 large onion, finely chopped
2 garlic cloves, finely crushed
1 cm/½ in fresh root ginger, bruised
2 litres/3½ pints/8 cups beef or
    chicken stock, including soaking liquid
    from the mushrooms
30 ml/2 tbsp soy sauce
115 g/4 oz curly kale, spinach or
    Chinese leaves (Chinese cabbage),
    shredded

1 First prepare the meatballs. Mix the beef with the onion, garlic, cornflour and seasoning in a food processor and then bind with sufficient egg white to make a firm mixture. With wetted hands, roll into tiny, bite-size balls and set aside.

2 Drain the mushrooms and reserve the soaking liquid to add to the stock. Trim off and discard the stalks. Slice the caps finely and set aside.

3 Heat a wok or large pan and add the oil. Fry the onion, garlic and ginger to bring out the flavour, but do not allow to brown.

4 When the onion is soft, pour in the stock with the reserved soaking liquid from the mushrooms. Bring to the boil, then stir in the soy sauce and mushroom slices and simmer for 10 minutes. Add the meatballs and cook for a further 10 minutes.

5 Just before serving, remove the ginger. Stir in the shredded curly kale, spinach or Chinese leaves. Heat through for 1 minute only but no longer or the leaves will be over-cooked. Serve the soup immediately.

COOK'S TIP: Any unused fresh root ginger will keep very well in the freezer provided it is left unpeeled and well-wrapped in freezer-foil.

11

Meatball & Pasta Soup

This soup from sunny Sicily is substantial enough for a hearty supper.

Serves 4

INGREDIENTS

1 very thick slice of white bread, crusts
  removed
30 ml/2 tbsp milk
225 g/8 oz/2 cups minced (ground) beef
1 garlic clove, crushed
30 ml/2 tbsp finely grated Parmesan cheese
30–45 ml/2–3 tbsp fresh flat leaf
  parsley leaves, coarsely chopped
1 egg
nutmeg, for grating

FOR THE SOUP

2 x 300 g/11 oz cans condensed
  beef consommé
90 g/3½ oz/scant 1 cup dried very thin pasta,
  broken into small pieces
fresh flat leaf parsley, to garnish
freshly grated Parmesan cheese, to serve
salt and freshly ground black pepper

1 Make the meatballs. Break the bread into a small bowl, add the milk and set aside to soak. Put the minced beef, garlic, Parmesan, parsley and egg in another bowl. Grate nutmeg over the top and season to taste.

2 Squeeze the bread with your hands to remove as much milk as possible, then add to the meatball mixture and mix well. Form the mixture into balls the size of small marbles.

3 Tip the consommé into a large pan, add water as directed on the labels, then add an extra can of water. Season to taste and bring to the boil.

4 Drop in the meatballs and add the pasta. Bring to the boil, stirring gently. Simmer for 7–8 minutes. Serve hot sprinkled with parsley and Parmesan.

Nutty Chicken Balls

Serve as a first course with the sauce or make smaller balls for canapés.

Serves 4

INGREDIENTS
350 g/12 oz/3 cups minced (ground) raw
  chicken
50 g/2 oz/½ cup pistachio nuts, chopped
15 ml/1 tbsp lemon juice
2 eggs, beaten
flour, for shaping
75 g/3 oz/¾ cup blanched chopped almonds
75 g/3 oz/generous 1 cup dried breadcrumbs
salt and freshly ground black pepper

FOR THE LEMON SAUCE
150 ml/¼ pint/⅔ cup chicken stock
225 g/8 oz/1 cup cream cheese
15 ml/1 tbsp lemon juice
15 ml/1 tbsp chopped fresh parsley
15 ml/1 tbsp snipped fresh chives

1 Make the meatballs. Mix the chicken with seasoning, the pistachio nuts, lemon juice and one beaten egg.

2 Shape into 16 balls with floured hands. Roll the balls in the remaining beaten egg and coat with the almonds and then the dried breadcrumbs. Chill until ready to cook.

3 Preheat the oven to 190°C/375°F/ Gas 5. Place on a greased baking tray and bake for about 15 minutes.

4 To make the lemon sauce, gently heat the chicken stock and cream cheese together in a pan, whisking until smooth. Add the lemon juice, herbs and season to taste.

Chicken Cigars

These small, crispy rolls can be served warm as canapés with a drink before a meal, or as a first course with a crisp, colourful salad.

Serves 4

INGREDIENTS
1 x 275 g/10 oz packet of filo pastry,
    thawed if frozen
45 ml/3 tbsp olive oil
fresh parsley, to garnish

FOR THE FILLING
15 ml/1 tbsp olive oil
1 small onion, finely chopped
350 g/12 oz/3 cups minced (ground) raw
    chicken
1 egg, beaten
2.5 ml/½ tsp ground cinnamon
2.5 ml/½ tsp ground ginger
30 ml/2 tbsp raisins
salt and freshly ground black pepper

2 Preheat the oven to 180°C/350°F/ Gas 4. Once the filo pastry packet has been opened, keep the pastry covered at all times with a damp dish towel. Work fast, as the pastry dries out very quickly when exposed to the air. Unravel the pastry and cut into 10 x 25 cm/4 x 10 in strips.

1 Heat the oil for the filling in a large frying pan and cook the onion until tender. Set aside to cool. Meanwhile mix all the remaining filling ingredients together in a bowl. Add the cooled onion to the mixture.

3 Take one strip, covering the remaining pastry. Brush with a little oil and place a small spoonful of filling about 1 cm/½ in from the end.

4 To encase the filling, fold the sides inwards to a width of 5 cm/2 in and roll into a cigar shape. Place on a greased baking tray and brush with oil. Bake for about 20–25 minutes, until golden brown and crisp. Garnish with fresh parsley.

Lettuce-wrapped Garlic Lamb

For this tasty starter, lamb is stir-fried with garlic, ginger and spices, then served in crisp lettuce leaves with yogurt, lime pickle and mint leaves.

Serves 4

INGREDIENTS
450 g/1 lb lamb fillet
2.5 ml/½ tsp chilli powder
10 ml/2 tsp ground coriander
5 ml/1 tsp ground cumin
2.5 ml/½ tsp ground turmeric
30 ml/2 tbsp groundnut oil
3–4 garlic cloves, chopped
15 ml/1 tbsp grated fresh root ginger
150 ml/¼ pint/⅔ cup lamb stock or water
4–6 spring onions (scallions), sliced
30 ml/2 tbsp chopped fresh coriander
   (cilantro)
15 ml/1 tbsp lemon juice
lettuce leaves, yogurt, lime pickle
   and mint leaves, to serve

2 In a bowl mix together the chilli powder, ground coriander, cumin and turmeric. Add the lamb and rub the spice mixture into the meat. Cover and leave to marinate for about 1 hour.

3 Heat the oil in a preheated wok. When hot, add the garlic and ginger and allow to sizzle for a few seconds.

1 Trim the lamb fillet of any fat and cube into small pieces, then mince in a blender or food processor, taking care not to over-process so that you retain some texture.

4 Add the lamb and continue to stir-fry for 2–3 minutes. Pour in the stock or water and continue to stir-fry until all the liquid has been absorbed and the lamb is tender, adding a little more stock or water, if necessary.

5 Add the spring onions, fresh coriander and lemon juice. Stir-fry for 30–45 seconds. Serve with the lettuce, yogurt, pickle and mint.

VARIATION: Vegetables, such as cooked diced potatoes or peas, can be added to the mince.

Dolmades

These dainty vine leaf parcels are very popular in Mediterranean countries. They are traditionally served as part of a Greek mezze.

Serves 4

INGREDIENTS
8 vine leaves
green and red (bell) pepper salad,
    to serve

FOR THE FILLING
15 ml/1 tbsp olive oil
115 g/4 oz/1 cup minced (ground) beef
30 ml/2 tbsp pine nuts
1 onion, chopped
15 ml/1 tbsp chopped fresh coriander
    (cilantro)
5 ml/1 tsp ground cumin
15 ml/1 tbsp tomato purée
salt and freshly ground black pepper

FOR THE TOMATO SAUCE
150 ml/¼ pint/⅔ cup passata
150 ml/¼ pint/⅔ cup beef stock
10 ml/2 tsp caster (superfine) sugar

1 For the filling, heat the oil in a pan. Add the minced beef, pine nuts and onion. Cook for 5 minutes.

2 Stir in the fresh coriander, cumin and tomato purée. Cook for a further 3 minutes and season well.

3 Lay a vine leaf, shiny side down, on a work surface. Place some filling in the centre of the leaf and fold the stalk end over the filling. Roll the parcel up towards the tip of the leaf and place in a lightly greased flameproof dish, seam side down. Fill the other leaves.

VARIATION: If vine leaves are unavailable, use lettuce or cabbage leaves blanched in boiling water until wilted.

4 For the sauce, mix together the passata, stock and sugar and pour over each vine leaf. Cover and cook on a moderate heat for 3–4 minutes. Reduce the heat and cook for a further 30 minutes. Serve with green and red pepper salad.

Fish Bites with Crispy Cabbage

Add an exotic element to a special meal with these attractive and tasty fish bites, which are sure to impress.

Serves 4

INGREDIENTS
FOR THE FISH BITES
350 g/12 oz/1½ cups peeled prawns (shrimp)
350 g/12 oz cod fillet, skinned and checked
    for bontes
10 ml/2 tsp light soy sauce
10 ml/2 tsp sesame seeds
oil for deep frying
spring onion (scallion) brushes, to garnish

FOR THE CABBAGE
225 g/8 oz Savoy cabbage
5 ml/1 tsp caster (superfine) sugar
pinch of salt
15 g/½ oz/1 tbsp flaked almonds
soy sauce, to serve

2 Roll the mixture into 16 even-size balls and toss in the sesame seeds to coat all over, pressing on firmly.

3 Heat the oil for deep-frying to 160°C/325°F. Shred the cabbage and place in the hot oil. Fry for 2 minutes. Drain well then sprinkle the cabbage with the sugar and some salt and toss in the flaked almonds. Keep warm.

1 Put the prawns and cod in a food processor and process for 20 seconds. Place in a large bowl and stir in the soy sauce.

VARIATION: Any firm, white fish, such as haddock or whiting would make a good substitute for cod.

4 Fry the balls in two batches for 5 minutes, until golden brown. Remove with a draining spoon. Serve, garnished with spring onion brushes, with the cabbage and some spring roll sauce for dipping.

Little Chicken Pies

These crisp little pies are equally delicious hot or cold and are perfect for packed lunches and picnics.

Makes 35

INGREDIENTS
225 g/8 oz/2 cups strong white bread flour
2.5 ml/½ tsp salt
2.5 ml/½ tsp caster (superfine) sugar
5 ml/1 tsp easy-blend dried yeast
25 g/1 oz/2 tbsp butter, softened
1 egg, beaten, plus a little extra
90 ml/6 tbsp warm milk
fresh parsley, to garnish

FOR THE FILLING
1 small onion, finely chopped
175 g/6 oz/1½ cups minced (ground)
    raw chicken
15 ml/1 tbsp sunflower oil
75 ml/5 tbsp chicken stock
30 ml/2 tbsp chopped fresh parsley
pinch of grated nutmeg
salt and freshly ground black pepper

1 Sift the flour, salt and sugar into a large bowl. Stir in the dried yeast, then make a well in the centre.

2 Add the butter, egg and milk and mix to a soft dough. Turn on to a lightly floured surface and knead for 10 minutes, until smooth and elastic.

3 Put the dough in a clean bowl, cover with clear film and leave in a warm place to rise for 1 hour, or until the dough has doubled in bulk.

4 Meanwhile, fry the onion and chicken in the oil for 10 minutes. Add the stock and simmer for 5 minutes. Stir in the parsley, nutmeg and salt and pepper. Leave to cool.

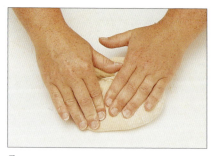

5 Preheat the oven to 220°C/425°F/ Gas 7. Knead the dough, then roll out until 3 mm/⅛ in thick. Stamp out rounds with a 7.5 cm/3 in cutter.

VARIATION: Left-over Christmas turkey could be used instead of chicken – omit the nutmeg and add 15 ml/1 tbsp of curry paste with the parsley and seasoning.

6 Brush the edges with beaten egg. Put a little filling in the middle, then press the edges together. Leave to rise on oiled baking sheets, covered with oiled clear film, for 15 minutes. Brush with a little more egg. Bake for 5 minutes, then for 10 minutes at 190°C/375°F/Gas 5, until well risen. Serve garnished with fresh parsley.

Dim Sum

Popular as a Chinese snack, these tiny dumplings are fast becoming fashionable in many restaurants.

Serves 4

INGREDIENTS

FOR THE DOUGH
150 g/5 oz/1¼ cups plain (all-purpose) flour
50 ml/2 fl oz/¼ cup boiling water
25 ml/1½ tbsp cold water
7.5 ml/½ tbsp vegetable oil

FOR THE FILLING
75 g/3 oz/¾ cup minced (ground) pork
45 ml/3 tbsp chopped canned
   bamboo shoots
7.5 ml/½ tbsp light soy sauce
5 ml/1 tsp dry sherry
5 ml/1 tsp demerara (raw) sugar
2.5 ml/½ tsp sesame oil
5 ml/1 tsp cornflour (cornstarch)

TO SERVE
lettuce leaves, such as iceberg,
   or Little Gem (Bibb)
soy sauce
spring onion (scallion) curls
sliced red chilli
prawn (shrimp) crackers

1 For the dough, sift the flour into a bowl. Stir in the boiling water, then the cold water with the oil. Mix to form a dough and knead until smooth.

2 Divide the mixture into 16 equal-size pieces and shape each piece into a small circle.

3 For the filling, mix together the pork, bamboo shoots, soy sauce, sherry, sugar and oil. Add the cornflour.

4 Place a little of the filling in the centre of each dim sum circle. Pinch the edges of the dough together to form little parcels.

VARIATION: Substitute cooked peeled prawns (shrimp) for the pork. Sprinkle 15 ml/1 tbsp of sesame seeds on to the dim sum before cooking in the steamer.

5 Line a steamer with a damp dish towel. Place the dim sum in the steamer and steam for 5–10 minutes. Serve on a bed of lettuce with soy sauce, spring onion curls, sliced red chilli and prawn crackers.

Indian Curried Lamb Samosas

In India, these snacks are a way of life – sold from stalls lining the streets of towns and villages throughout the country.

Serves 4

INGREDIENTS
15 ml/1 tbsp oil
1 garlic clove, crushed
175 g/6 oz/1½ cups minced (ground) lamb
4 spring onions (scallions), finely chopped
10 ml/2 tsp medium curry paste
4 ready-to-eat dried apricots, chopped
1 small potato, diced
10 ml/2 tsp apricot chutney
30 ml/2 tbsp frozen peas
dash of lemon juice
15 ml/1 tbsp fresh chopped coriander
    (cilantro)
225 g/8 oz puff pastry, thawed if frozen
beaten egg, to seal and glaze
5 ml/1 tsp cumin seeds
salt and freshly ground black pepper
45 ml/3 tbsp natural yogurt and
    15 ml/1 tbsp chopped fresh mint,
    to serve
fresh mint sprigs, to garnish

1 Preheat the oven to 220°C/425°F/ Gas 7 and dampen a large, non–stick baking sheet.

2 Heat the oil in a frying pan and fry the garlic for 30 seconds, then add the lamb. Continue frying for about 5 minutes, stirring frequently, until the meat is well browned.

3 Stir in the spring onions, curry paste, apricots and potato, and cook for 2–3 minutes. Add the apricot chutney, peas and 60 ml/4 tbsp water. Cover and simmer for 10 minutes, stirring occasionally. Stir in the lemon juice and chopped coriander. Season, remove from the heat and leave to cool.

4 On a floured surface, roll out the pastry and cut into 15 cm/6 in squares. Place a quarter of the curry mixture in the centre of each pastry square and brush the edges with beaten egg. Fold over to make a triangle and seal the edges. Mark the edges with the back of a knife and make a small slit in the top of each.

VARIATION: Filo pastry can be used instead of puff pastry; in which case, the samosas should be deep fried in oil until golden brown.

5 Brush each samosa with beaten egg and sprinkle over the cumin seeds. Place on the damp baking sheet and bake for 20 minutes. Serve with yogurt and mint, garnished with mint sprigs.

Spicy Meat Fritters

Quick and easy, these delicious fritters would make a light summer lunch, served with plain rice and salad.

Makes 30

INGREDIENTS
450 g/1 lb potatoes, boiled
   and drained
450 g/1 lb/4 cups lean minced (ground) beef
1 onion, quartered
1 bunch spring onions (scallions), chopped
3 garlic cloves, crushed
5 ml/1 tsp ground nutmeg
15 ml/1 tbsp coriander seeds, dry roasted
   and ground
10 ml/2 tsp cumin seeds, dry fried
   and ground
4 eggs, beaten
oil for shallow frying
salt and freshly ground
   black pepper
fresh coriander (cilantro) leaves,
   to garnish

1 While the potatoes are still warm, mash them in the pan until they are well broken up. Add to the minced beef in a bowl and mix well together.

2 Finely chop the onion, spring onions and garlic. Add to the minced beef mixture, together with the ground nutmeg, coriander and cumin. Stir in enough beaten egg to give a soft consistency which can be formed into fritters. Season to taste with salt and pepper.

3 Heat the oil in a large frying pan. Using a dessertspoon, scoop out 6–8 oval-shaped fritters and drop them into the hot oil. Allow to set, so that they keep their shape (this will take about 3 minutes) and then turn over and cook for a further minute.

4 Drain well on kitchen paper and keep warm while cooking the remaining fritters. Serve hot, garnished with fresh coriander.

VARIATION: A mixture of half beef and half pork could be used instead of beef.

COOK'S TIP: Dry frying whole spices helps to bring out their full aroma and flavour. Heat a heavy-based frying pan and add the coriander and cumin seeds. Fry, stirring constantly, for about 30 seconds, until the spices begin to give off their aroma. Remove the pan from the heat and leave to cool, then grind the seeds in a spice grinder, a coffee grinder kept expressly for this purpose or crush in a mortar with a pestle.

Balti Chicken with Chillies

This stir-fried dish is cooked in a matter of minutes and makes a very economical family supper.

Serves 4

INGREDIENTS

275 g/10 oz boned and cubed skinless
   chicken breast
2 thick red chillies
3 thick green chillies
45 ml/3 tbsp corn oil
6 curry leaves
3 medium onions, sliced
7.5 ml/1½ tsp crushed garlic
7.5 ml/1½ tsp ground coriander (cilantro)
7.5 ml/1½ tsp finely grated fresh
   root ginger
5 ml/1 tsp chilli powder
5 ml/1 tsp salt
15 ml/1 tbsp lemon juice
30 ml/2 tbsp chopped fresh
   coriander (cilantro) leaves
chapatis and lemon wedges, to serve

1 Boil the chicken cubes in water for about 10 minutes, until soft and cooked through. Drain.

2 Place the chicken in a food processor to mince. Take care not to over-process or the chicken will become too pulpy.

3 Cut the chillies in half lengthways and remove the seeds, if desired. Cut the flesh into strips.

4 Heat the oil in a wok or frying pan and fry the curry leaves and onions until the onions are golden brown. Lower the heat; add the garlic, coriander, ginger, chilli powder and salt.

5 Add the chicken and stir-fry over a medium heat for 3–5 minutes, until the chicken begins to colour.

COOK'S TIP: Taste this dish during cooking as it is quite mild and may need additional spices to suit some palates.

6 Add the lemon juice, the chilli strips and most of the fresh coriander leaves. Stir for a further 3–5 minutes, then serve at once, garnished with the remaining coriander leaves and accompanied by chapatis and lemon wedges.

Lebanese Kibbeh

The national dish of Syria and the Lebanon is kibbeh, made from minced lamb and bulgur wheat.

Serves 6

INGREDIENTS
115 g/4 oz/¾ cup bulgur wheat
450 g/1 lb/4 cups minced (ground) lean lamb
1 large onion, grated
15 ml/1 tbsp melted butter
salt and freshly ground black pepper
sprigs of mint, to garnish
rice, to serve

FOR THE FILLING
30 ml/2 tbsp oil
1 onion, finely chopped
225 g/8 oz/2 cups minced (ground) lamb
50 g/2 oz/½ cup pine nuts
2.5 ml/½ tsp ground allspice

FOR THE YOGURT DIP
600 ml/1 pint/2½ cups Greek yogurt
2–3 garlic cloves, crushed
15–30 ml/1–2 tbsp chopped fresh mint

1 Preheat the oven to 190°C/375°F/ Gas 5. Rinse the bulgur wheat in a sieve and squeeze out excess moisture.

2 Mix the lamb, onion and seasoning, kneading to make a thick paste. Add the bulgur wheat and blend together.

3 To make the filling, heat the oil in a frying pan and fry the onion until golden. Add the lamb or veal and cook, stirring, until evenly browned and then add the pine nuts, allspice and salt and pepper.

4 Oil a large ovenproof dish and spread half the meat and bulgur wheat mixture over the bottom. Spoon over the filling and top with a second layer of meat and bulgur wheat, pressing down firmly with the back of a spoon.

5 Pour the melted butter over the top and then bake in the oven for 40–45 minutes, until browned on top.

6 Meanwhile, make the yogurt dip: blend together the yogurt and garlic, spoon into a serving bowl and sprinkle with the chopped mint.

7 Cut the cooked kibbeh into squares or rectangles and serve garnished with mint and accompanied by rice and the yogurt dip.

Moussaka

Kefalotiri, a hard, sharp cheese made with sheep's or goat's milk, makes the perfect flavouring in this topping for a classic moussaka.

Serves 6

INGREDIENTS
2 large aubergines (eggplants), thinly sliced
45 ml/3 tbsp olive oil
675 g/1½ lb/6 cups lean minced (ground) beef
1 onion, chopped
2 garlic cloves, crushed
2 large fresh tomatoes, chopped, or 200 g/7 oz canned chopped tomatoes
120 ml/4 fl oz/½ cup dry white wine
45 ml/3 tbsp chopped fresh parsley
45 ml/3 tbsp fresh breadcrumbs
2 egg whites
salt and freshly ground black pepper

FOR THE TOPPING
40 g/1½ oz/3 tbsp butter
40 g/1½ oz/⅓ cup plain (all-purpose) flour
400 ml/14 fl oz/1⅔ cups milk
2.5 ml/½ tsp freshly grated nutmeg
150 g/5 oz/1¼ cups grated Kefalotiri cheese
2 egg yolks, plus 1 whole egg

1 Layer the aubergines in a colander, sprinkling each layer with salt. Drain over a sink for 20 minutes, then rinse and pat dry with kitchen paper.

2 Preheat the oven to 190°C/375°F/ Gas 5. Spread out the aubergines in a roasting pan. Brush with olive oil, then bake for 10 minutes, until just softened. Set aside. Leave the oven on.

3 Make the meat sauce. Heat the remaining olive oil in a large pan and brown the minced beef, stirring frequently. When the meat is no longer pink and looks crumbly, add the onion and garlic and cook for 5 minutes.

4 Add the tomatoes to the pan and stir in the wine. Season with salt and pepper to taste. Bring to the boil, then lower the heat, cover and simmer for 15 minutes. Remove the pan from the heat, leave to cool for about 10 minutes, then stir in the chopped parsley, fresh breadcrumbs and the egg whites.

5 Lightly grease a large ovenproof dish, then spread out half the sliced aubergines in an even layer on the base. Spoon over the meat sauce, spread it evenly, then top with the remaining aubergines.

6 To make the topping, put the butter, flour and milk in a medium pan. Bring to the boil over a low heat, whisking all the time until the mixture thickens to form a smooth, creamy sauce. Lower the heat and simmer for 2 minutes. Remove the pan from the heat, season, then stir in the nutmeg and half the cheese.

7 Cool for 5 minutes, then beat in the egg yolks and the whole egg. Pour the sauce over the aubergine topping and sprinkle with the remaining cheese. Bake for 30–40 minutes, or until golden brown. Allow the dish to stand for 10 minutes before serving.

Stilton Burgers

Slightly more up-market than the traditional burger, this tasty recipe contains a delicious surprise – lightly melted tangy Stilton cheese encased in the crunchy burger.

Serves 4

INGREDIENTS
450 g/1 lb/4 cups minced (ground) beef
1 onion, finely chopped
1 celery stick, chopped
5 ml/1 tsp dried mixed herbs
5 ml/1 tsp prepared mustard
50 g/2 oz/½ cup crumbled
    Stilton cheese
4 burger buns
salt and freshly ground black pepper
salad and mustard pickle, to serve

1 Place the minced beef in a bowl, together with the onion and celery. Season well.

2 Stir in the herbs and mustard, bringing all the ingredients together to form a firm mixture.

3 Divide the mixture into eight equal portions. Place four on a chopping board and flatten each one slightly.

4 Place the crumbled Stilton cheese in the centre of each, dividing it equally among them.

5 Flatten the remaining portions and place on top. Mould the mixture together encasing the crumbled cheese and shape into four burgers.

6 Grill (broil) under a medium heat for 10 minutes, turning once or until cooked through. Split the burger buns and place a burger and salad leaves inside each. Serve with salad and mustard pickle.

Spaghetti Bolognese

This dish was adapted by Italian émigrés to America in the Sixties.

Serves 4–6

INGREDIENTS
30 ml/2 tbsp olive oil
1 onion, finely chopped
1 garlic clove, crushed
5 ml/1 tsp dried mixed herbs
1.5 ml/¼ tsp cayenne pepper
350–450 g/12 oz–1 lb/3–4 cups minced
    (ground) beef
400 g/14 oz can chopped tomatoes
45 ml/3 tbsp tomato ketchup
15 ml/1 tbsp sun-dried tomato paste
5 ml/1 tsp Worcestershire sauce
5 ml/1 tsp dried oregano
450 ml/¾ pint/scant 2 cups beef stock
45 ml/3 tbsp red wine
400–450 g/14 oz–1 lb dried spaghetti
salt and freshly ground black pepper
freshly grated Parmesan cheese, to serve

1 Heat the oil in a medium pan and cook the onion and garlic over a low heat, stirring frequently, for about 5 minutes. Stir in the herbs and cayenne and cook for 2–3 minutes. Add the beef and cook, stirring frequently, for about 5 minutes.

2 Stir in the tomatoes, ketchup, tomato paste, Worcestershire sauce, oregano and seasoning. Add the stock and red wine. Bring to the boil, stirring. Cover and simmer for 30 minutes, stirring often.

3 Cook the pasta according to the instructions on the packet. Drain and divide among warmed bowls. Taste the sauce and adjust the seasoning, then spoon it on top of the pasta and sprinkle with a little grated Parmesan.

Beef-stuffed Peppers

Spicy mince makes a delightful change from a rice-based stuffing.

Serves 4

INGREDIENTS
4 red (bell) peppers
1 onion
2 celery sticks
450 g/1 lb/4 cups minced (ground) lean beef
60 ml/4 tbsp olive oil
50 g/2 oz button (white) mushrooms
pinch of ground cinnamon
salt and freshly ground black pepper
chervil or flat leaf parsley,
    to garnish
green salad, to serve

1 Cut the tops off the peppers and reserve. Remove the seeds and membranes from the peppers. Finely chop the onion and celery. Set aside.

2 Sauté the beef in a non-stick frying pan for a few minutes, stirring until it is no longer red. Transfer the beef to a plate. Add half the oil to the pan and sauté the onion and celery over a high heat until the onion starts to brown.

3 Add the mushrooms and stir in the partly cooked beef. Season with the cinnamon, salt and pepper. Cook over a low heat for about 30 minutes.

4 Preheat the oven to 190°C/375°F/ Gas 5. Cut a sliver off the base of each pepper so they stand level, spoon in the beef mixture and replace the lids. Arrange in an oiled ovenproof dish, drizzle over the oil and cook for 30 minutes. Serve with green salad.

Cottage Pie

A great family favourite, cottage pie is almost a meal in itself and needs little in the way of accompanying vegetables.

Serves 4

INGREDIENTS
50 g/2 oz/4 tbsp butter
1 large onion, finely chopped
1 celery stalk, finely diced
1 large carrot, finely diced
450 g/1 lb/4 cups lean minced (ground) beef
15 ml/1 tbsp flour
250 ml/8 fl oz/1 cup hot beef stock
30 ml/2 tbsp chopped fresh parsley
15 ml/1 tbsp tomato purée (paste)
900 g/2 lb floury potatoes
45–60 ml/3–4 tbsp milk
10 ml/2 tsp spicy brown mustard
salt and freshly ground black pepper

2 Sprinkle the flour evenly over the surface and stir it into the meat and vegetable mixture.

3 Gradually add the stock, stirring well. Stir in the parsley and tomato purée. Season with salt and pepper. Bring to a simmer, then cover and cook over a very low heat, stirring occasionally, for 45 minutes.

1 Melt 15 g/½ oz/1 tbsp of the butter in a frying pan over a moderate heat. Add the onion, celery and carrot and cook until the onion is soft, stirring occasionally. Add the beef and fry, stirring, until it is brown and crumbly.

VARIATION: For shepherd's pie, substitute lamb for beef. If time allows, prepare the mince and leave to cool before topping with the cooled mashed potatoes.

4 Meanwhile, cook the potatoes in boiling salted water until they are tender. Drain well. Transfer to a bowl and mash them. Add the remaining butter and just enough milk to make a soft fluffy texture. Season to taste with plenty of salt and pepper. Preheat the oven to 200°C/400°F/Gas 6.

5 Stir the mustard into the beef mixture, then turn it into an ovenproof dish. Cover with a neat layer of potatoes and seal to the sides of the dish. Mark with a fork, if liked. Bake for 20–25 minutes. Serve hot.

Meat Loaf with Mushroom Stuffing

This variation of the ever-popular meat loaf is just as filling, but has an extra touch of elegance.

Serves 6

INGREDIENTS

25 g/1 oz/2 tbsp butter
225 g/8 oz mushrooms, coarsely chopped
1 small onion, finely chopped
130 g/4½ oz/2¼ cups fresh breadcrumbs
45 ml/3 tbsp chopped fresh parsley
5 ml/1 tsp dried thyme
10 ml/2 tsp bottled brown sauce
675 g/1½ lb/6 cups lean minced (ground) beef
225 g/8 oz/2 cups lean minced (ground) pork
75 ml/5 tbsp tomato ketchup
2 eggs, beaten
salt and freshly ground black pepper
flat leaf parsley, to garnish
tomatoes and steamed asparagus, to serve

1 Preheat the oven to 190°C/375°F/ Gas 5. Melt the butter in a large frying pan. Cook the mushrooms and onion in the butter over a moderate heat until soft. Turn the mixture into a large bowl.

2 Add the breadcrumbs, parsley, thyme, brown sauce, salt and pepper to the mushrooms. Mix well.

3 In another bowl, mix the beef with the pork, tomato ketchup and eggs, and plenty of salt and pepper.

4 Pack half the meat mixture into a large loaf tin, pressing it into an even layer. Pack the mushroom mixture on top, then cover with the rest of the meat. Bake for 1¼ hours.

5 Remove from the oven and leave to stand for 15 minutes. Pour off the juices, then turn out the meat loaf on to a serving plate. Garnish with parsley and serve with tomatoes and asparagus, if wished.

COOK'S TIP: Meat loaf is perfect for packed lunches or picnics as when it is cold it can be cut into firm slices that go well with crusty bread and chutney or pickles.

Lasagne

This classic pasta dish is made with layers of lasagne, Bolognese sauce and a creamy béchamel sauce, topped with cheese.

Serves 4–6

INGREDIENTS
about 12 sheets dried lasagne
1 quantity Bolognese sauce (see
    Spaghetti Bolognese)
about 50 g/2 oz/½ cup freshly grated
    Parmesan cheese
tomato slices and parsley sprig, to garnish

BECHAMEL SAUCE
900 ml/1½ pints/3¾ cups whole milk
1 onion, 1 carrot, stick of celery, sliced
few whole peppercorns
50 g/2 oz/4 tbsp butter
75 g/3 oz/⅔ cup plain (all-purpose) flour
freshly grated nutmeg
salt and freshly ground black pepper

1 First make the béchamel sauce. Pour the milk into a saucepan and add the vegetables and peppercorns. Bring to boiling point, remove from the heat and set aside to infuse for at least 30 minutes.

2 Strain the milk into a jug. Melt the butter in the same saucepan and stir in the flour. Cook, stirring, for 2 minutes.

3 Remove from the heat and add the milk all in one go, whisk well and return to the heat. Bring to the boil, whisking all the time, then simmer for 2–3 minutes, stirring constantly until thickened. Season to taste with salt, pepper and nutmeg.

4 Preheat the oven to 180°C/350°F/Gas 4. If necessary, cook the sheets of lasagne in plenty of boiling salted water according to the instructions. Lift out with a slotted spoon and drain on a clean tea towel. Spoon one-third of the meat sauce into a buttered ovenproof dish.

5 Cover the meat sauce with sheets of lasagne and spread with one-third of the béchamel sauce. Repeat twice more, finishing with a layer of béchamel sauce covering the whole top.

6 Sprinkle with Parmesan cheese and bake in the oven for 45 minutes, until brown. Serve garnished with tomato slices and a sprig of parsley.

SPECIAL OCCASION DISHES

Fish Balls with Chinese Vegetables

These tasty fish balls are easy to make using a food processor. Here they are partnered with a selection of green vegetables.

Serves 4

INGREDIENTS
FOR THE FISH BALLS
450 g/1 lb white fish fillets, skinned, boned and cubed
3 spring onions (scallions), chopped
1 lean back bacon rasher (strip), rinded and chopped
15 ml/1 tbsp Chinese rice wine
30 ml/2 tbsp light soy sauce
1 egg white
fresh coriander, to garnish

FOR THE VEGETABLES
1 small head pak choi
5 ml/1 tsp cornflour (cornstarch)
15 ml/1 tbsp light soy sauce
150 ml/¼ pint/⅔ cup fish stock
30 ml/2 tbsp groundnut oil
2 garlic cloves, sliced
2.5 cm/1 in piece fresh root ginger, cut into thin shreds
75 g/3 oz green beans
175 g/6 oz mangetouts (snow peas)
3 spring onions (scallions), sliced diagonally into 5–7.5 cm/2–3 in lengths
salt and freshly ground black pepper

1 Put the fish, spring onions, bacon, rice wine, soy sauce and egg white in a food processor. Process until smooth. Form the mixture into about 24 balls.

2 Steam the fish balls in batches in a lightly greased bamboo steamer set over a wok for 5–10 minutes, until firm. Remove from the steamer and keep warm.

3 Meanwhile, trim the pak choi, removing any discoloured leaves or damaged stems, then tear into manageable pieces.

4 In a small bowl blend together the cornflour, soy sauce and stock to a smooth paste. Set aside.

5 Heat the oil in a preheated wok and swirl it around. Add the garlic and ginger and stir-fry for 1 minute. Add the beans and stir-fry for 2–3 minutes, then add the mangetouts, spring onions and pak choi. Stir-fry for 2–3 minutes.

6 Add the sauce to the wok and cook, stirring, until it has thickened and the vegetables are tender but crisp. Taste and adjust the seasoning, if necessary. Serve with the fish balls, garnished with coriander.

Chicken & Apricot Filo Pie

The filling for this pie has a Middle-Eastern flavour – minced chicken combined with apricots, bulgur wheat, nuts and spices.

Serves 6

INGREDIENTS
75 g/3 oz/½ cup bulgur wheat
75 g/3 oz/6 tbsp butter
1 onion, chopped
450 g/1 lb/4 cups minced (ground) raw
  chicken
50 g/2 oz/¼ cup dried apricots, chopped
25 g/1 oz/¼ cup blanched almonds, chopped
5 ml/1 tsp ground cinnamon
2.5 ml/½ tsp ground allspice
50 ml/2 fl oz/¼ cup Greek yogurt
15 ml/1 tbsp snipped fresh chives
30 ml/2 tbsp chopped fresh parsley
6 sheets filo pastry, thawed if frozen
salt and freshly ground black pepper
chives, to garnish

1 Preheat the oven to 200°C/400°F/ Gas 6. Put the bulgur wheat in a bowl with 120 ml/4 fl oz/½ cup boiling water. Soak for 5–10 minutes, until the water is absorbed. Heat 25 g/1 oz/ 2 tbsp of butter and fry the onion and chicken until pale golden.

2 Stir in the apricots, almonds and bulgur wheat and cook for a further 2 minutes. Remove from the heat and stir in the cinnamon, allspice, yogurt, chives and parsley. Season to taste with salt and pepper.

3 Melt the remaining butter. Unroll the filo pastry and cut into 25 cm/ 10 in rounds. Keep the pastry rounds covered with a clean, damp dish towel to prevent them drying.

4 Line a 23 cm/9 in loose-based flan tin with three of the pastry rounds, brushing each one with butter as you layer them.

5 Spoon the chicken mixture into the tin and spread evenly, then cover this with three more pastry rounds, brushing each round with melted butter as before.

6 Crumple the remaining rounds and place them on top of the pie, then brush over any remaining melted butter. Bake the pie for about 30 minutes until the pastry is golden brown and crisp. Serve hot or cold, cut in wedges and garnished with chives.

Risotto

An Italian dish made with short grain arborio rice which gives a creamy consistency to this easy one-pan recipe.

Serves 4

INGREDIENTS

15 ml/1 tbsp oil
175 g/6 oz/1½ cups arborio rice
1 onion, chopped
225 g/8 oz/2 cups minced (ground) raw
    chicken
600 ml/1 pint/2½ cups chicken stock
1 red (bell) pepper, seeded and chopped
1 yellow (bell) pepper, seeded and chopped
75 g/3 oz frozen green beans
115 g/4 oz chestnut mushrooms, sliced
15 ml/1 tbsp chopped fresh parsley
salt and freshly ground black pepper
fresh parsley, to garnish

1 Heat the oil in a large frying pan. Add the rice and cook for 2 minutes, until transparent.

2 Add the onion and minced chicken. Cook for 5 minutes, stirring occasionally. Pour in the stock and bring to the boil. Stir in the peppers and reduce the heat. Cook for 10 minutes.

3 Add the green beans and mushrooms and cook for a further 10 minutes.

4 Stir in the fresh parsley and season well to taste. Cook for 10 minutes, or until the liquid has been absorbed. Serve, garnished with fresh parsley.

Beef & Mushroom Meatballs

The rich acidity of Roquefort sauce enhances the flavour of these deeply-flavoured meatballs. Serve with buttered ribbon pasta.

Serves 4

INGREDIENTS

15 g/½ oz/¼ cup dried ceps, soaked in
   warm water for 20 minutes
450 g/1 lb/4 cups lean minced (ground) beef
1 small onion, finely chopped
2 egg yolks
10 ml/2 tsp chopped fresh thyme
30 ml/2 tbsp olive oil
celery salt and freshly ground black pepper

FOR THE ROQUEFORT SAUCE

200 ml/7 fl oz/scant 1 cup whole milk
50 g/2 oz/½ cup walnuts, toasted
3 slices white bread, crusts removed
75 g/3 oz Roquefort cheese
60 ml/4 tbsp chopped fresh parsley

1 Drain the mushrooms, reserving the liquid, and chop finely. Place the beef, onion, egg yolks, thyme and seasoning in a bowl, add the mushrooms and combine. Roll into small balls.

2 Make the sauce. Place the milk in a pan and bring to a simmer. Grind the walnuts in a food processor, add the bread, milk, reserved liquid, cheese and parsley, then process smoothly. Transfer to a bowl, cover and keep warm.

3 Heat the olive oil in a large non-stick frying pan. Cook the meatballs for 6–8 minutes. Add the sauce and heat very gently, without allowing to boil. Serve with ribbon pasta.

51

Meatballs with Peperonata

These taste very good with creamed potatoes. Use a potato ricer to get them really smooth.

Serves 4

INGREDIENTS
400 g/14 oz/3½ cups minced (ground) beef
115 g/4 oz/2 cups fresh white breadcrumbs
50 g/2 oz/⅔ cup grated Parmesan cheese
2 eggs, beaten
pinch of paprika
pinch of grated nutmeg
5 ml/1 tsp dried mixed herbs
2 thin slices of mortadella or prosciutto (total weight about 50 g/2 oz), chopped
vegetable oil, for shallow frying
salt and freshly ground black pepper
snipped fresh basil leaves, to garnish

FOR THE PEPERONATA
30 ml/2 tbsp olive oil
1 small onion, thinly sliced
2 yellow (bell) peppers, cored, seeded and cut lengthways into thin strips
2 red (bell) peppers, cored, seeded and cut lengthways into thin strips
275 g/10 oz/1¼ cups finely chopped tomatoes or passata
15 ml/1 tbsp chopped fresh parsley

1 Put the minced beef in a bowl. Add half the breadcrumbs and all the remaining ingredients, except the oil and basil leaves. Mix well with clean wet hands. Divide the mixture into 12 equal portions and roll each into a ball. Flatten the meatballs so they are about 1 cm/½ in thick.

2 Put the remaining breadcrumbs on a plate and roll the meatballs in them, a few at a time, until they are evenly coated. Place on a plate, cover with clear film and chill for about 30 minutes to firm up.

3 Meanwhile, make the peperonata. Heat the oil in a medium pan, add the onion and cook gently for about 3 minutes, stirring frequently, until softened. Add the pepper strips and cook for a further 3 minutes, stirring constantly.

4 Stir in the tomatoes or passata and parsley, with salt and pepper to taste. Bring to the boil, stirring. Cover and cook for 15 minutes, then remove the lid and continue to cook, stirring frequently, for 10 minutes more, or until reduced and thick. Taste for seasoning. Keep hot.

5 Pour oil into a frying pan to a depth of about 2.5 cm/1 in. When hot but not smoking, shallow fry the meatballs for 10–12 minutes, turning three or four times and pressing them flat with a fish slice. Remove and drain on kitchen paper. Serve hot, with the peperonata alongside. Garnish with the basil.

Lion's Head Meatballs

These larger-than-usual pork meatballs are first fried, then simmered in stock. They are traditionally served with a fringe of greens, such as pak choi, to represent the lion's mane.

Serves 2–3

INGREDIENTS

450 g/1 lb/4 cups lean pork, minced (ground)
   finely with a little fat
4–6 drained canned water chestnuts,
   finely chopped
5 ml/1 tsp finely chopped fresh
   root ginger
1 small onion, finely chopped
30 ml/2 tbsp dark soy sauce
beaten egg, to bind
30 ml/2 tbsp cornflour (cornstarch), seasoned
   with salt and freshly ground black pepper
30 ml/2 tbsp groundnut oil
300 ml/½ pint/1¼ cups chicken stock
2.5 ml/½ tsp sugar
115 g/4 oz pak choi, stalks trimmed
   and the leaves rinsed
salt and freshly ground black pepper

1 Mix the pork, water chestnuts, ginger and onion with 15 ml/1 tbsp of the soy sauce in a bowl. Add salt and pepper to taste, stir in enough beaten egg to bind, then form into eight or nine balls. Toss a little of the cornflour into the bowl and make a paste with the remaining cornflour and water.

2 Heat the oil in a large frying pan and brown the meatballs all over. Using a slotted spoon, transfer the meatballs to a wok or deep frying pan.

3 Add the stock, sugar and the remaining soy sauce to the oil that is left in the pan. Heat gently, stirring to incorporate the sediment on the bottom of the pan. Pour over the meatballs, cover and simmer gently for 20–25 minutes.

4 Increase the heat and add the pak choi. Continue to cook for 2–3 minutes, or until the leaves are just wilted.

5 Lift out the greens and arrange on a serving platter. Top with the meatballs and keep hot. Stir the cornflour paste into the sauce. Bring to the boil, stirring, until it thickens. Pour over the meatballs and serve at once.

VARIATION: Crab meat or prawns can be used instead of some of the pork in this recipe. Alternatively, you could try substituting minced lamb or beef for the minced pork used here.

Fish Cakes

For special fish cakes, you could use a mix of fresh and smoked salmon.

Serves 4

INGREDIENTS
450 g/1 lb/15⅓ cups cooked,
    mashed potatoes
450 g/1 lb/4 cups cooked mixed white
    and smoked fish such as haddock
    or cod, flaked
25 g/1 oz/2 tbsp butter, diced
45 ml/3 tbsp chopped fresh parsley
1 egg, separated
1 egg, beaten
about 50 g/2 oz/scant 1 cup fine
    dry breadcrumbs
vegetable oil, for frying
freshly ground black pepper
mixed salad, to serve

1 Place the potatoes in a bowl and beat in the fish, butter, parsley and egg yolk. Season with pepper.

2 Divide the fish mixture into eight equal portions, then, with floured hands, form each into a flat cake.

3 Beat the remaining egg white with the whole egg. Dip each fish cake in beaten egg, then in breadcrumbs.

4 Heat the oil in a frying pan, then fry the fish cakes for about 3–5 minutes on each side, until crisp and golden. Drain on kitchen paper and serve hot with a mixed salad.

Best-ever Burgers

Once you have tried home-made burgers you will never want any others.

Serves 4

INGREDIENTS
15 ml/1 tbsp vegetable oil
1 small onion, finely chopped
450 g/1 lb/4 cups minced (ground) beef
1 large garlic clove, crushed
5 ml/1 tsp ground cumin
10 ml/2 tsp ground coriander
30 ml/2 tbsp tomato purée (paste) or ketchup
5 ml/1 tsp wholegrain mustard
dash of Worcestershire sauce
30 ml/2 tbsp chopped fresh mixed herbs
   (parsley, thyme and oregano or marjoram)
15 ml/1 tbsp lightly beaten egg
flour, for shaping
oil, for frying (optional)
salt and freshly ground black pepper
mixed salad, fries and relish, to serve

1 Heat the oil in a frying pan, add the onion and cook for 5 minutes. Remove from the pan, drain on kitchen paper and leave.

2 Mix together the beef and next eight ingredients. Season to taste. Stir in the onions.

3 Sprinkle a board with flour and shape the mixture into four burgers. Cover and chill for 15 minutes.

4 Heat the oil in a pan and fry the burgers for about 5 minutes on each side, depending on how rare you like them, or cook under a medium grill for the same time. Serve with salad, fries and relish.

Koftas in Pitta Pockets

These Turkish meatballs are made with minced lamb and flavoured with the favourite Middle-Eastern flavours of cumin and mint.

Serves 4

INGREDIENTS

1 slice bread
225 g/8 oz/2 cups minced (ground) lamb
1 garlic clove, crushed
1 small onion, finely chopped
5 ml/1 tsp ground cumin
15 ml/1 tbsp chopped fresh mint
15 ml/1 tbsp pine nuts
flour for coating
oil for shallow frying
4 pitta breads
1 onion, cut into thin rings
2 tomatoes, sliced or cut
    into wedges
salt and freshly ground black pepper
fresh mint, to garnish

1 Preheat the oven to 220°C/425°F/ Gas 7. Soak the bread in water for 5 minutes, then squeeze dry and add to the next six ingredients. Season. Mix until blended and malleable. Shape into small balls, using dampened hands so that the mixture does not stick. Coat in flour.

2 Shallow fry the koftas in oil for about 6 minutes, turning frequently, until golden brown.

3 Heat the pitta breads in the oven, then cut a thin strip off one side to make a pocket. Fill each bread with onion rings, tomato wedges and a few koftas Serve garnished with mint.

Mexican Tacos

Ready-made taco shells make perfect edible containers for shredded salad, spicy beef, grated cheese and sour cream.

Serves 4

INGREDIENTS

15 ml/1 tbsp olive oil
250 g/9 oz/generous 2 cups lean minced
   (ground) beef
1 garlic clove, crushed
5 ml/1 tsp ground cumin
5–10 ml/1–2 tsp mild chilli powder
8 ready-made taco shells
½ small iceberg lettuce, shredded
1 small onion, thinly sliced
2 tomatoes, chopped in chunks
1 avocado, halved, stoned
   and sliced
60 ml/4 tbsp sour cream
115 g/4 oz/1 cup grated Cheddar or
   Monterey Jack cheese
salt and freshly ground black pepper

1 Heat the oil in a frying pan. Add the meat, with the garlic and spices, and brown over a medium heat, stirring frequently to break up any lumps. Season, cook for 5 minutes, then set aside to cool slightly.

2 Meanwhile, warm the taco shells according to the instructions on the packet. Do not let them get too crisp. Spoon the lettuce, onion, tomatoes and avocado slices into the taco shells. Top with the sour cream followed by the minced beef mixture.

3 Sprinkle the cheese into the tacos and serve immediately. Tacos are eaten with the fingers, so have plenty of paper napkins handy.

Popovers

Great fun and full of goodness, these individual corn Yorkshire puddings are filled with tasty meat patties and then baked.

Serves 4

INGREDIENTS
50 g/2 oz/½ cup plain (all-purpose) flour
pinch of salt
1 egg
150 ml/¼ pint/⅔ cup whole milk
50 g/2 oz/½ cup canned sweetcorn, drained
15 g/½ oz/1 tbsp butter
cooked vegetables, or salad, to serve

FOR THE FILLING
115 g/4 oz/1 cup minced (ground) beef
1 red onion, chopped
30 ml/2 tbsp tomato relish
50 g/2 oz/1 cup fresh wholemeal
   breadcrumbs
15 ml/1 tbsp oil
salt and freshly ground black pepper

1 Preheat the oven to 220°C/425°F/ Gas 7. For the batter, sift the flour and salt into a mixing bowl. Make a well in the centre.

2 Whisk the egg into the flour mixture, add the milk gradually to form a smooth batter. Add the sweetcorn.

3 For the filling, place the minced beef in a large bowl. Add the onion and seasoning.

4 Stir in the tomato relish and breadcrumbs and bring the mixture together. Roll into four patties.

5 Heat the oil in a large pan and fry the patties to seal. Place the butter in a four-section Yorkshire pudding tin and put into the preheated oven until melted.

6 Divide the batter among each section of the tin and place a patty in the centre of each. Cook for 30 minutes. Remove from the oven and serve with freshly cooked vegetables, or salad.

Beef Pasties

Ever popular, these meat and vegetable filled parcels may be made in advance and frozen.

Serves 8

INGREDIENTS
15 ml/1 tbsp oil
175 g/6 oz/1½ cups minced (ground) beef
15 ml/1 tbsp tomato purée (paste)
1 onion, chopped
1 carrot, diced
50 g/2 oz turnip, diced
1 large potato, diced
25 g/1 oz/¼ cup flour
150 ml/¼ pint/⅔ cup beef stock
15 ml/1 tbsp chopped fresh parsley
450 g/1 lb prepared shortcrust pastry
1 egg, beaten
salt and freshly ground black pepper
salad, to serve

2 Stir in the flour and cook for 1 minute. Stir in the stock and season to taste. Cook over a gentle heat for 10 minutes. Stir in the fresh parsley and leave to cool.

3 Roll out the pastry to a large rectangle. Cut eight 15 cm/6 in circles, using a bowl or saucer as a template.

1 Preheat the oven to 190°C/375°F/Gas 5. Heat the oil in a large pan and add the minced beef. Cook for 5 minutes. Stir in the tomato purée, onion, carrot, turnip and potato. Cook for a further 5 minutes.

VARIATION: Use the same quantity of minced turkey instead of the beef and substitute sliced celery for the turnip. Replace the beef stock with chicken stock.

4 Spoon the filling on to one half of each pastry circle, brush the edges with egg and fold in half to form a semi-circle. Crimp the edges and roll. Brush the pasties with egg and place on a baking sheet. Cook for 35 minutes or until golden. Serve with a crisp salad.

Index

This edition is published by Lorenz Books, an imprint of Anness Publishing Ltd, 108 Great Russell Street, London WC1B 3NA info@anness.com www.annesspublishing.com; twitter: @Anness_Books

© Anness Publishing Limited 2015

If you like the images in this book and would like to investigate using them for publishing, promotions or advertising, please visit our website www.practicalpictures.com for more information.

Publisher: Joanna Lorenz
Editor: Valerie Ferguson & Helen Sudell
Production Controller: Pirong Wang

Recipes contributed by: Catherine Atkinson, Angela Boggiano, Lesley Chamberlain, Maxine Clarke, Trisha Davies, Roz Denny, Joanna Farrow, Sarah Gates, Shirley Gill, Carole Handslip, Deh-Ta Hsuing, Shehzad Husain, Judy Jackson, Soheila Kimberley, Norma MacMillan, Sue Maggs, Sallie Morris,

Jenny Stacey, Hilaire Walden, Steven Wheeler, Jeni Wright.
Photography: Edward Allwright, Steve Baxter, Mickie Dowie, James Duncan, Ian Garlick, Michelle Garrett, John Heseltine, Amanda Heywood, Ferguson Hill, Janine Hosegood, David Jordan, William Lingwood, Patrick McLeavey.

A CIP catalogue record for this book is available from the British Library

COOK'S NOTES

Bracketed terms are intended for American readers.

For all recipes, quantities are given in both metric and imperial measures and, where appropriate, in standard cups and spoons. Follow one set of measures, but not a mixture.

Standard spoon and cup measures are level. 1 tsp = 5ml, 1 tbsp = 15ml, 1 cup = 250ml/ 8fl oz. Australian standard tablespoons are 20ml. Australian readers should use 3 tsp in place of 1 tbsp for measuring small quantities.

American pints are 16fl oz/2 cups. American readers should use 20fl oz/2.5 cups in place of 1 pint when measuring liquids.

Electric oven temperatures in this book are for conventional ovens. When using a fan oven, the temperature will probably need to be reduced by about 10–20°C/20–40°F. Check with your manufacturer's instruction book for guidance.

Medium (US large) eggs are used unless otherwise stated.